ARE THERE REALLY TIGERS IN TIGER BAY?

AND OTHER ANIMAL POEMS

WRITTEN BY HAZEL HOULDEY

AuthorHouse™ UK
1663 Liberty Drive
Bloomington, IN 47403
www.authorhouse.com
Phone: 1 (800) 839-8640

Published by AuthorHouse   11/17/2017

ISBN: 978-1-5462-8499-4 (sc)
ISBN: 978-1-5462-8498-7 (e)

Print information available on the last page.

Any people depicted in stock imagery provided by Thinkstock are models,
and such images are being used for illustrative purposes only.
Certain stock imagery © Thinkstock.

This book is printed on acid-free paper.

authorHOUSE®

ARE THERE REALLY TIGERS IN TIGER BAY?

This book is dedicated to Basir and Jalal

Are there really tigers in Tiger Bay?

A little girl asked her Grandad one day

Oh yes of course, her Grandad said

As she settled her teddy bears to bed

This is how the story goes

He said, remembering all he knows

A ship came in one stormy night

In the bay it docked in pale moonlight

With giant sails that dripped with stars

And a crew with tattooed arms and scars

They said the ship was full of beasts

They travelled mysteriously from the east

Bound for a circus here in town

But once the heavy ropes were down

A tiger forced and broke his chain

Ran from his prison into the rain

Leapt high above the sailor's heads

Made a dash for freedom they said

The biggest cat they'd ever seen

Fled through the darkness like a dream

His paws as big as dinner plates

Flashing dagger teeth as he jumped the crates

Imagine on that evening's news

As everybody voiced their views

Shut your doors! Lock your locks!

Make sure you don't go near the docks!

He's very big and very clever

No one hardly sees him ever

Sometimes from the corner of your eye

You see a shape or shadow go by

This stripey prowler in her mind

One day she hoped she would find

There's been all sorts of stories told

About his sightings new and old

Someone once said he was found

Visiting the dragon in the castle grounds

Grandad said he's very glad

No one has caught him. That would be sad

Just before she went to sleep

Just as the stars began to peep

The little girl was very sure

She saw a shadow pass the door

Then outside the window frame

Did Grandad see it too the same?

She wasn't dreaming, Grandad knew

As long ago he'd seen it too

In a time when childhood hearts receive

A precious gift to still believe

In Tiger Bay just be aware

Keep a look out while you're there

You never know, you might just see

The Tiger bay tiger, just like me.

OTHER ANIMAL POEMS

THE SNAIL

As the snail
Leaves a trail
Of silver thread
He's so shy
If you try
To touch his head
He will hide
Safe inside
His carried shell
Like the snail
When we fail
We hide as well

MANATEE

If you're kind you may find
A manatee
As they roam, peaceful home
Of foamy sea
Sailors weaved, yarns believed
So long before
Some agree, a manatee
A mermaid pure

THE DODO

If you ever go to Mauritius
And see something quite suspicious
It'll only be the dodo bird
But he's extinct, that's quite absurd!
Ah yes but last night I had a dream
And thousands of dodos I had seen
Wandering around without a care
I hope that they are all still there.

HORSES HEAVEN

I woke up this morning
The sky was pink
And the last clouds fell away
from their broken link
Then thoughts began to tumble
Like beads from a thread
Colouring my heart
As they scatter in my head

Then I want to take my horse
And just gallop away
To lost horizons
To a whole new day
I want to take my horse
Just ride and ride
To where the moon
hangs like a shell
To the peaceful tide

When pressures get too heavy
My shoulders bear the weight
When I feel so weary
And I can't think straight
I yearn for the presence
Of my trusted steed
I know he'll be swift
To answer my need

He's as strong as Bucephalus
With a mane of silk
And eyes like gemstones
In pools of milk
I feel so safe
As he carries me
Then we fly like Pegasus
On wind and sea

And I'll take my horse
And I'll gallop away
To lost horizons
To a whole new day
I'll take my horse
I'll ride and ride
To where the moon
hangs like a shell
To the peaceful tide

To horses heaven on
the peaceful tide

SHOEBILL

The shoebill was created
With such a funny face
No peacock feathers
Or swan grace
But a stilted walk
And a distant call
So unique is the shoebill after all
Some people have said
What an ugly bird!
I don't think so
But don't take my word
When you have some time
Go and take a look
I'm sure you can find one somewhere in a book
So spare the shoebill a little thought
Think how he would feel if he was caught
And faced with us humans You can never tell
He'd probably think
We look funny as well!

ANIMAL ADVENTURE

I sat on a rock with a python
And soaked up all the sun
Then laughed with a hyena
Over something funny he'd done

A gnu told me some stories
The best I've ever heard
Then I took down some shorthand
With a secretary bird

I played cards with a cheetah
He won the game of course
I swam in a deep long river
With a giant river horse

I saw a leopard hiding
In the shade of a leafy tree
The elephant quickly spotted her
And called her in for tea

I saw an impala dancing
Just by herself in the moon
She was asked if she'd like company
By a very well mannered baboon

I said goodnight to a zebra
My pyjamas striped just like him
I read the monkeys a bedtime story
And one by one tucked them in.

FRIENDSHIP BUTTERFLY

On gentle wings
Cloud brushed with sun and rain
Come join together in peace
These flowers of harmony
Soft butterfly
Show all sweet pastures
That wait for them
To grow
Even when their petals sigh
To earth
They're only sleeping
Awaiting a new birth.

ARACHNID

Spider spin your web of silky thread for me
Every strand being woven with your skill
There to be admired by all who watches
And as each season turns you're spinning still
Spider you will teach your children all you do
They will carry on then just the same
Your works will be displayed in many places
Against many a background, patterned or plain
Spider go on with your endless weaving
Let the breeze play music with each strand
Clinging to your web of life forever
Never to be broken, proud and grand

TWILIGHT OWL

Silent wings
Softly sweeping, gliding, sighing
A feathered breath in flight
The owl of twilight
Gently, earthly, slumber inviting
A murmur on the wing
The all seeing eyes
Jewels in the dark
A soundless journey
A dance in dusk
Graceful aviator
Keeper of night
A harp hardly touched in the orchestra.

THE HERON

Angel wing tips brushing lakes
A gliding dagger with sun drops gleam
Far beyond your blue, white, grey
Your eyes see days in the haven of trees I watched you
My heart wished to borrow your wings
To sail, to shiver through misted souls
To beat, to fly
Where peace and freedom sings
And bathe in music of whispering leaves.

LITTLE LAMB

Little Lamb born in the snow
Blessed with a voice all pastures know
Oh gifted life, oh gentle form
Sleep sweetly in your mother's song

Little lamb skip free and wild
Pure fleecy light soft valley child
A purple lake deep in your eyes
Rest in the womb of nature skies

Little lamb sing all the land
In prayer forever understand
A carefree gambolling in daybreak
I celebrate thee like William Blake.

Lightning Source UK Ltd.
Milton Keynes UK
UKRC02n2121091217
314151UK00002B/40